Arthur's Favourite Hymns

Easy to play
versions of favourite hymns including
spirituals
carols
hymns
and
sacred songs

With Thoughts for the Day
by Arthur Goddard

Arranged for piano and guitar by
Paul R Goddard

© Clinical Press Limited 2017

All rights reserved. No part of this publication may be reproduced, stored in a retrieval system, or transmitted in any form or by any means, electronic, mechanical, photocopying, recording or otherwise, without prior permission of the copyright owner

While the advice and information in this book is believed to be true and accurate at the time of going to press, neither the authors, the editors, nor the publisher can accept legal responsibility for any errors of omissions that may be made. The publisher makes no warranty, express or implied, with respect to the material conatined herein

Published by: Clinical Press Ltd., Redland Green Farm, Redland, Bristol, BS6 7HF, UK.
Many thanks to *Thankyou Music** for permission to include **From Heaven You Came** by Graham Kendrick

British Library Cataloguing in Publication Data

Goddard A.F., Goddard P.R.

Arthur's Favourite Hymns and Thoughts for the Day

1.Hymns, Favourite

ISBN 978-1-85457-0925

Contents

	PAGE NUMBER
Frontispiece: *Gwynfynydd, Snowdonia (1960s)* and *Banff in the Rockies (2015)*	iv
Foreword: *Revd Rod Symmons*	v
Introduction	vi

HYMN OR SACRED SONG	HYMN NUMBER	THOUGHT FOR THE DAY	PAGE NUMBER
Amazing Grace	1	*The Grace of God*	1
All In The April Evening	2		2
And Can It Be?	3	*Editor's Note*	4
As With Gladness	4	*Gifts*	5
Away in a Manger	5		6
Blessed Assurance	6		7
Burdens Are Lifted At Calvary	7	*Calvary*	8
Dear Lord And Father Of Mankind	8		9
Down By The Riverside	9		10
From Heaven You Came	10	*Birthdays*	11
Guide Me O Thou Great Redeemer	11		12
How Great Thou Art	12	*God's Greatness*	13
His Eye is on the Sparrow	13		14
How Sweet the Name of Jesus Sounds	14	*Ten Titles for Jesus*	15
Just A Closer Walk With Thee	15		16
Love Makes It Easy	16		17
Love Comes Shining Through	17	*Editor's Note*	18
Michael Row The Boat Ashore	18		20
Nobody Know The Trouble I've Seen	19		21
Oh Little Town of Bethlehem	20		22
Oh When The Saints	21	*Who is a saint?*	23
Silent Night	22		24
Swing Low, Sweet Chariot	23	*The Milk of the Word*	25
Tell Out My Soul	24		26
The Lord's My Shepherd	25	*Shepherds and their sheep*	27
The King of Love	26		28
The Old Rugged Cross	27		29
There Is A Green Hill	28	*Green Hills*	30
There Will Be Peace In The Valley	29	*Editor's Note*	31
There Were Ninety and Nine	30		32
Thou Didst Leave Thy Throne	31		33
Wade in the Water	32		34
We Have An Anchor	33	*Editor's Note*	35
What A Friend We Have In Jesus	34	*Friends*	36
When I Survey The Wondrous Cross	35		37
		Surveying	38

Front Cover *Arthur as a choirboy*
Back Cover *Arthur as a leader in the Boys Brigade (Christ Church, West Croydon) and in three choirs*
 Arthur and Grace

Gwynfynydd, Snowdonia (1960s) (See page 30)

Banff in the Rockies (2015) (see pages 13 and 30)

FOREWORD

I was delighted to be asked to write a Foreword to this unusual collection of hymns and carols.

There are two distinctive features to the book. The first is that the music has been rearranged by Paul to make it easier to play for those in the earlier stages of learning the piano, and he has also included some simple guitar chords. As someone who struggled to learn the piano at an earlier age this is something that I would have found very helpful.

The other feature is that these hymns and carols were all favourites of Paul's father, Arthur. I imagine many people who pick up this book will have known Arthur and it seems to me that this collection, and the associated comments, wonderfully reflect Arthur's character.

I count it a real privilege to have got to know Arthur a little during his later years after his move to Bristol. Arthur always seemed to have a smile on his face, had an irrepressible love for life and a ready stock of stories to tell. His room in the residential care home where he lived was part shrine to his beloved Crystal Palace, but there was a greater passion in his heart that had shaped his whole life and continued to motivate him to the end - his love of Jesus. He had trusted his life to Christ at a young age and his faith shaped who he was and all that he did. He might have retired from his professional life as a surveyor, but he had never retired from 'surveying the wondrous cross', or from encouraging others to do the same.

This collection is shaped by his final years at the home, where he led services for other residents. Simple arrangements enabled a young pianist to accompany the hymns and the hymns included in this book are amongst those that were used at the services and the 'thoughts for the day' reflect the homilies that he gave.

I am sure that this book will bring great pleasure to many people and will keep alive the vision that motivated Arthur for so many years.

Rod Symmons

Revd Rod Symmons
The vicar of Redland Parish Church
Area Dean of the City of Bristol Deanery
Associate Faculty Member of Trinity College.

INTRODUCTION

The idea for this collection of hymns really started with my father, Arthur Goddard. From the age of six to ninety-six Arthur sang in choirs, originally as a choir boy and later as a bass in church choirs. Latterly he helped organise and sang in the Purley Male Voice Praise choir. In 2012, when, for health reasons, Arthur moved to Abbots Leigh Nursing Home in Bristol, he wished to continue witnessing and did so by instigating a service of worship at the home on Sunday mornings. Sometimes an experienced pianist was available to play the hymns chosen for the Sunday service but often this was not the case and a younger or less-practiced accompanist would struggle through the scores in the hymn books. Arthur asked me if I could simplify the hymns and this I did with over thirty hymns and carols keeping them true to the original harmonies but simplifying the keys and layout. At the service Arthur would give a short often humorous talk....his thought for the day. Some of these have been reproduced in this book.

Arthur particularly enjoyed the visits that his relatives and friends made to the home and the assistance at Abbots Leigh Manor Nursing Home of Gill, Kim, Donna, Sister Carol, Rev'd Rod Symmons (the vicar at Redland Green Parish Church), Rev'd Hester Jones, Rowan, Cathy, the manager and David the owner. And, of course all the other staff (I can't mention them all by name but he was grateful to everyone there).

The Purley Male Voice Choir made a trip from Croydon to the home at Abbots Leigh twice a year and Arthur enormously enjoyed their visits. This enjoyment was shared by the residents at the home and a special "thank you" is due to Allan Turner for organising the visits and driving the minibus on the very long and tiring journeys there and back.

About once a month Lois and myself would play favourite songs and hymns at the nursing home. At such times I would often play my latest compositions and Arthur was always very supportive and appreciative. I have therefore added two of my own compositions to this collection and included some spirituals that Arthur took pleasure in hearing. Please enjoy playing and singing the hymns.

All proceeds from the sale of this book are going to the charity, *Dr Jazz Charitable Funds*.

Paul R Goddard (Editor and Arranger)

NOTE

The inspiration for Arthur's thoughts for the day often came from the hymns he had chosen. The stories surrounding these hymns are told extremely well in:
- Amazing Grace, 366 Inspiring Hymns Stories for Daily Devotions by Kenneth W. Osbeck, Second Edition, Kregel Publications,
- Famous Hymns, Well loved hymns and their stories, compiled by Christopher Idle, published by Lion Publishing plc
- The Nation's Favourite Hymns, by Andrew Barr, Songs of Praise (BBC) Lion Publishing plc.

Many thanks to *Thankyou Music** for permission to include **From Heaven You Came** by Graham Kendrick and apologies to anybody who we should have obtained permission from but may have mistakenly neglected to do so.

*Adm. by Capitol CMG Publishing excl. UK & Europe, adm. by Integrity Music, part of the David C Cook family, songs@integritymusic.com

1
Amazing Grace

John Newton

2. 'Twas grace that taught my heart to fear,
   And grace my fears relieved;
   How precious did that grace appear
   The hour I first believed.

3. Through many dangers, toils and snares,
   I have already come;
   'Tis grace hath brought me safe thus far,
   And grace will lead me home.

4. When we've been there ten thousand years,
   Bright shining as the sun,
   We've no less days to sing God's praise
   Than when we'd first begun.

ARTHUR'S THOUGHT FOR THE DAY
THE GRACE OF GOD

John Newton (17256-1807), the writer of many hymns including Amazing Grace, followed his father to sea at eleven years of age. He was hardworking and studied whenever he could, teaching himself Latin and a thorough grasp of mathematics. Eventually he became the captain of a slave ship but the violent and coarse life he led appalled him.

During a violent storm Newton turned to God for help and his life changed completely. He left the sea and, supported by John Wesley, studied for the ministry. After some difficulty he was appointed to an Anglican Church in Olney in Buckinghamshire. John Newton felt that the services needed simple hymns rather than solely singing psalms. He co-operated with William Cowper and in 1779 produced the *Olney Hymns*. Verses 1 to 4 of *Amazing Grace* were included (verse 5 was added later by John P Rees). Newton never ceased to wonder at God's grace which changed his life completely.

Bibliography: The Nations Favourite Hymns, Andrew Barr

All In The April Evening

Hugh S Roberton

"Behold, the Lamb of God, who takes away the sin of the world!" John 1:29

3
And Can It Be?

EDITOR'S NOTE. We were looking through a hymn book together and Arthur chuckled with glee when we reached this hymn by Charles Wesley. A friend of his in the church congregation was called Anne Kennet. *'It's a knock, knock joke,'* he laughed. *'Knock knock, whose there? Anne Kennet. Anne Kennet who? Anne Kennet be.....'* So if you are still around, Anne, there is a free copy of this book waiting for you.

4
As With Gladness

William Chatterton Dix (1837-98) — Conrad Kocher (1786-1872)

2. As with joyful steps they sped,
Savior, to Thy lowly bed,
There to bend the knee before
Thee whom heaven and earth adore,
So may we with willing feet
Ever seek Thy mercy-seat!

3. As they offered gifts most rare
At Thy cradle, rude and bare,
So may we with holy joy,
Pure and free from sin's alloy,
All our costliest treasures bring,
Christ, to Thee, our heavenly King!

4. Holy Jesus, every day
Keep us in the narrow way;
And when earthly things are past,
Bring our ransomed souls at last
Where they need no star to guide,
Where no clouds Thy glory hide.

5. In the heavenly country bright
Need they no created light;
Thou its Light, its Joy, its Crown,
Thou its Sun which goes not down.
There forever may we sing
Alleluias to our King!

ARTHUR'S THOUGHT FOR THE DAY: *GIFTS*

At Christmas time most of us are lucky enough to receive presents. Some are welcome, some not so. Imagine the disappointment of receiving a present where the family have paid the first part but you have to pay the rest!! Some gifts are really bribes, and we can think here of Judas Iscariot or the false witnesses at Christ's trial. Some gifts are a bonus for hard work, or, in some cases, not such hard work. You can make your own mind up about bankers and about the existence or not of a free lunch.

We ask the children *'What would you like?'* Replies vary but the old song by a little girl is brought to mind: *'All I want for Christmas is my two front teeth.'* Nowadays the usual reply may be for the latest and most expensive toy.

What do you want for Christmas? Health? Money? But the greatest gift, free to all who choose to accept, is that of Eternal Life through God's Son, Jesus Christ. What a tragedy that so many reject, ignore or are apathetic towards this gift. Although they will sing carols they only use the occasion of Christmas to *'have a good time'* when accepting Christ as Saviour and Lord of their lives would bring them true and lasting joy.

5
Away in a Manger

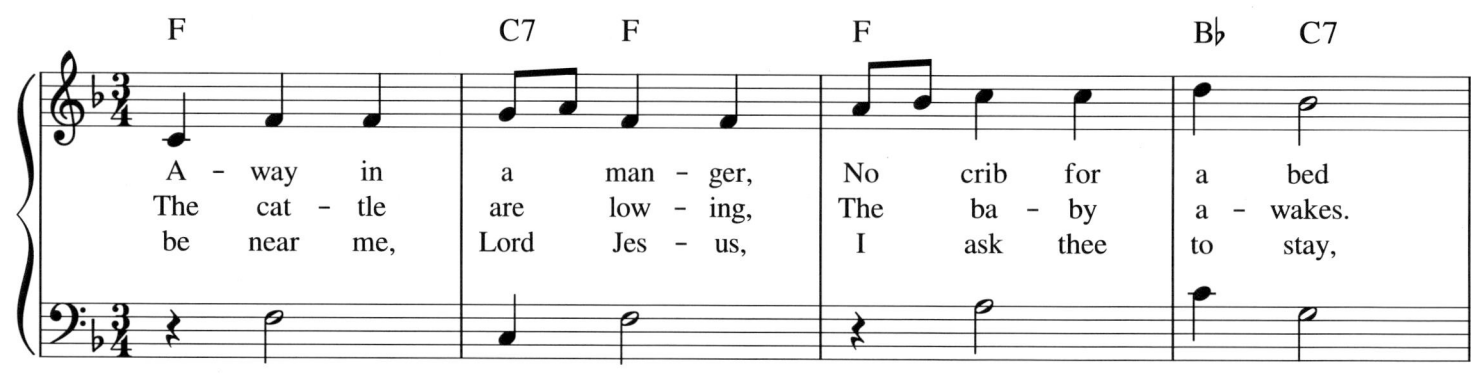
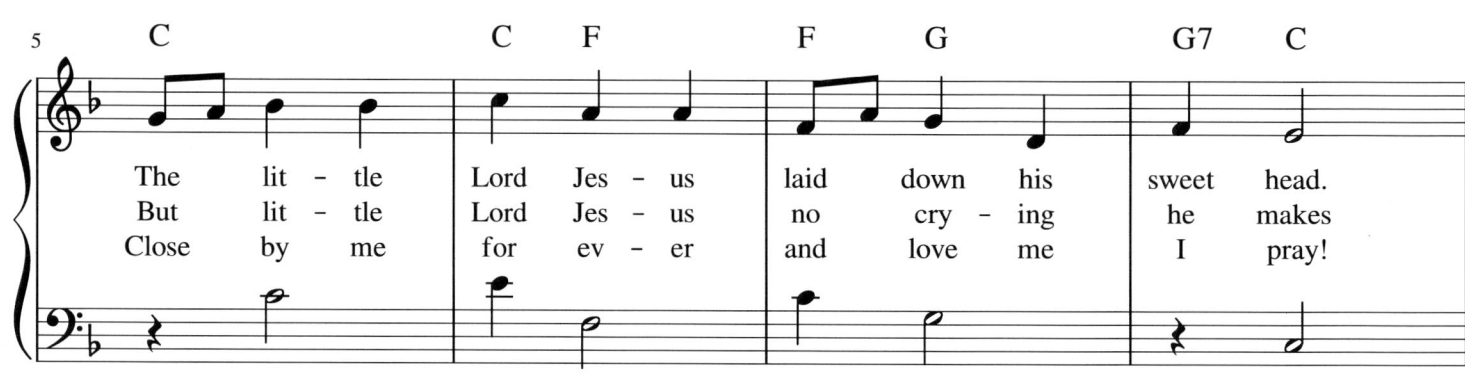
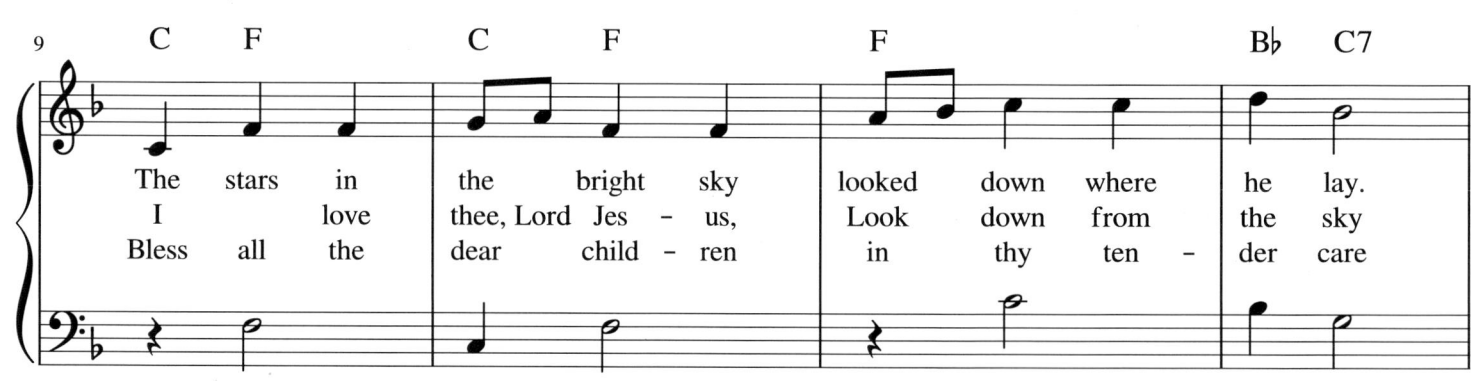
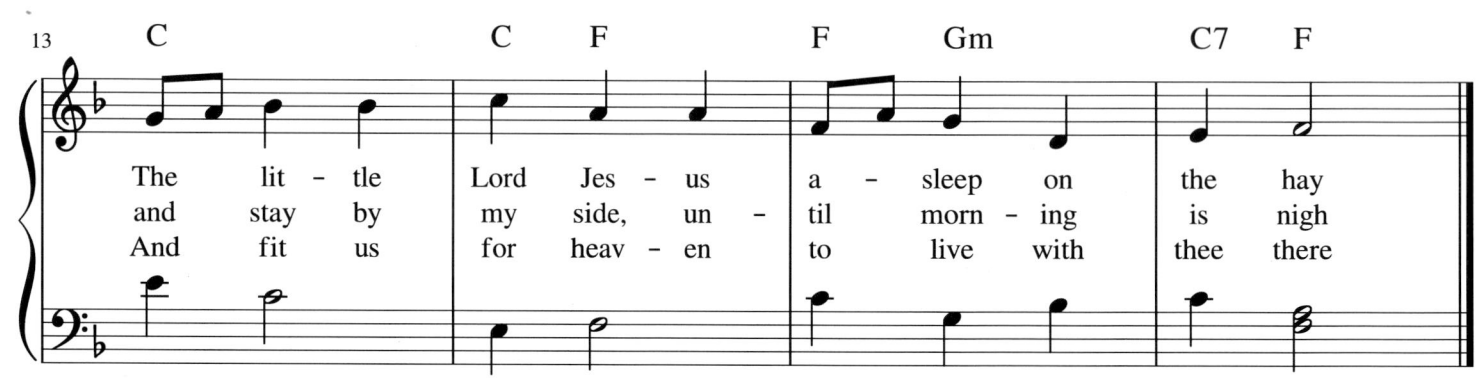

And she brought forth her firstborn son, and wrapped him in swaddling clothes, and laid him in a manger; because there was no room for them in the inn.

Luke 2:7 King James Version (KJV)

6
Blessed Assurance

Fanny J. Crosby Mrs. J.F. Knapp

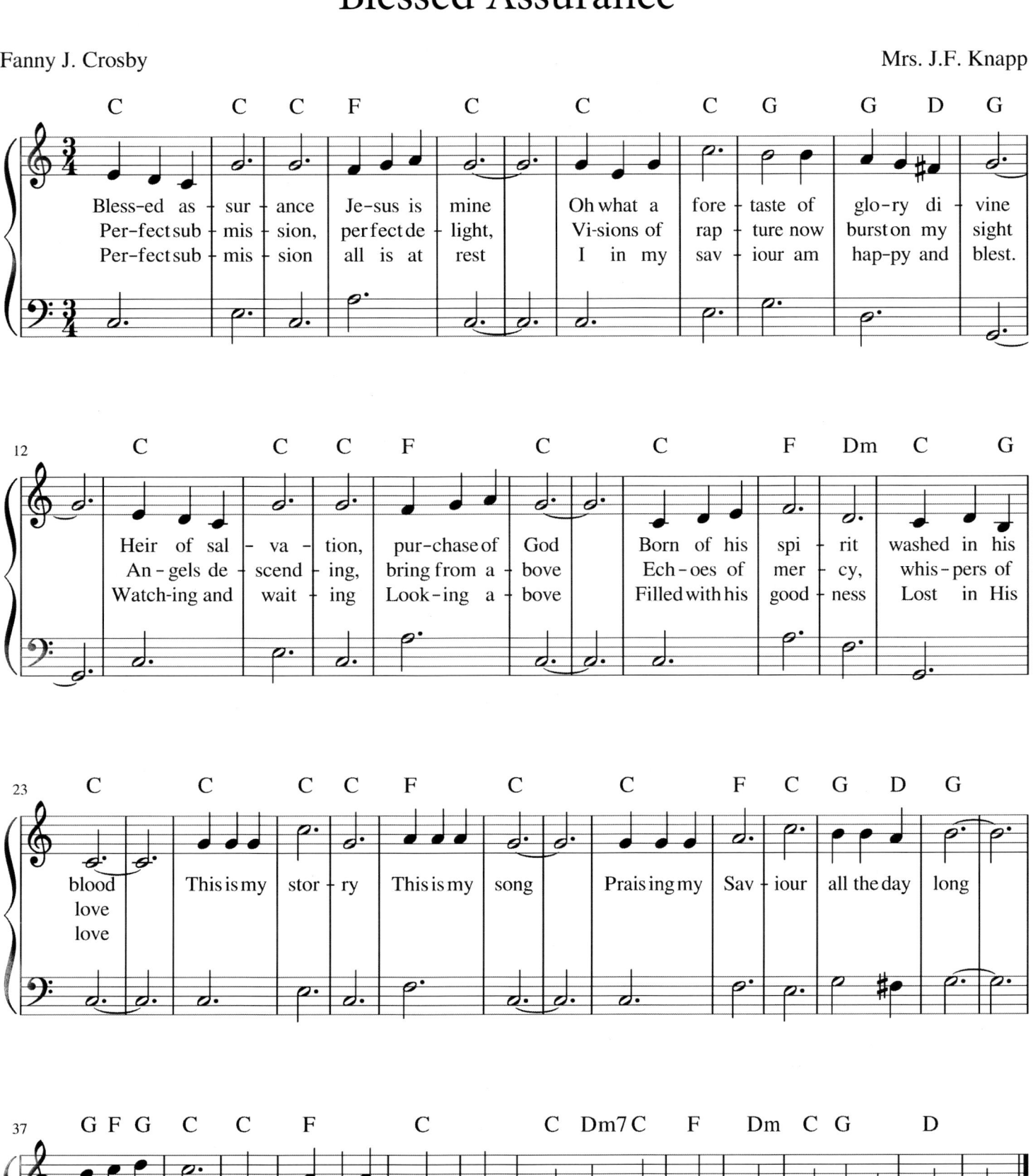

Let us hold unswervingly to the hope we profess, for he who promised is faithful.
Hebrews 10:23 New International Version (NIV)

7
Burdens Are Lifted At Calvary

ARTHUR'S THOUGHT FOR THE DAY:
CALVARY

This hymn was written by John Moore when he was assistant superintendent at the Seaman's chapel in Glasgow, Scotland. The company secretary of a shipping firm asked him to visit a seriously ill merchant seaman who was being treated in a Glasgow hospital. John Moore visited the seaman and during his conversation with the seaman took out a tract about Pilgrims's Progress by John Bunyan. This showed a pilgrim with a huge burden on his back. Moore explained that this had been his experience and that when he came to the cross of Jesus Christ the forgiveness had lifted a huge burden of sin from his own back. He asked if the seaman felt the burden of sin on his own back and the seaman had nodded his agreement. They had prayed together and the seaman had afterwards expressed his joy and relief that the burden had been lifted.

John Moore had returned home and later that night had written the hymn *"Burdens are lifted at calvary, Jesus is very near."*

The hymn has been such a blessing and help to me. and many people throughout the world

Bibliography

Amazing Grace: 366 Inspiring Hymn Stories for Daily Devotions © 2002 by Kenneth W. Osbeck. Published by Kregel Publications, Grand Rapids, MI.

8
Dear Lord And Father Of Mankind

Whittier   Parry

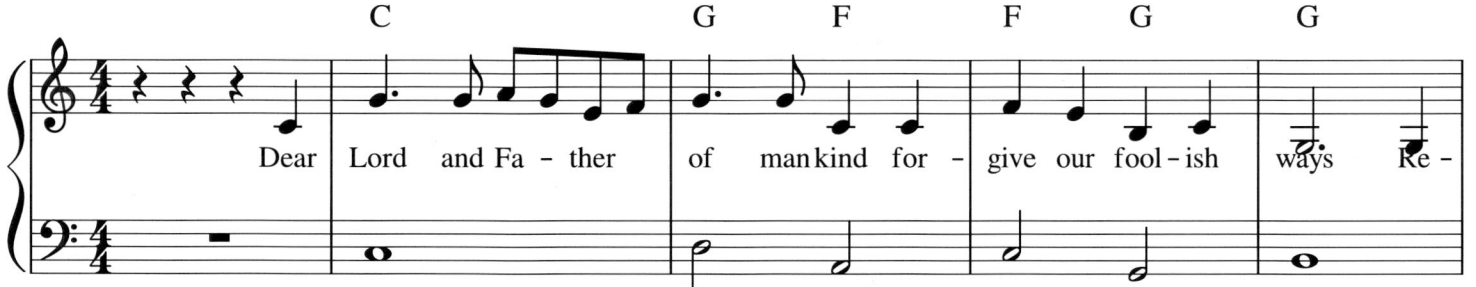

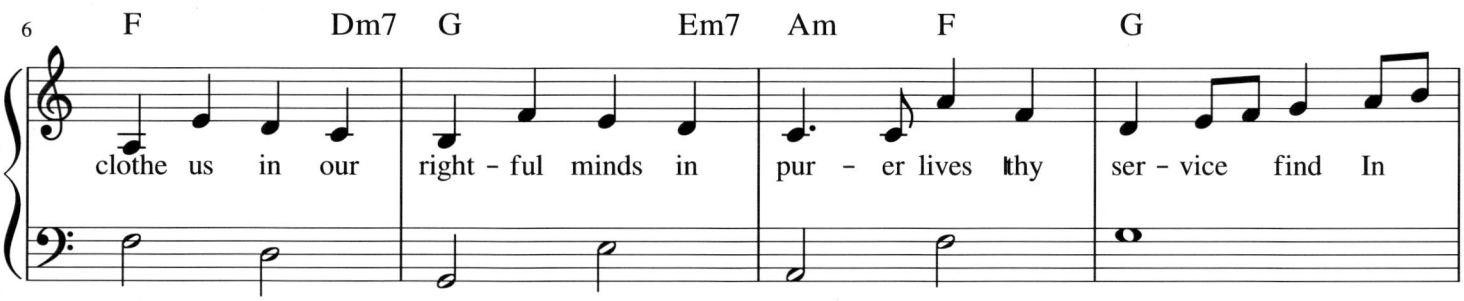

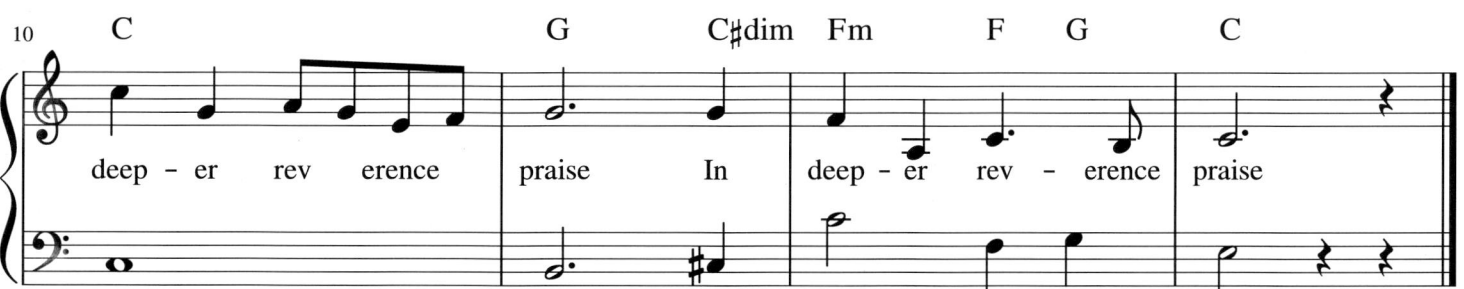

2.
In simple trust like theirs who heard,
Beside the Syrian sea,
The gracious calling of the Lord,
Let us, like them, without a word,
Rise up and follow thee.
Rise up and follow thee.

3.
O sabbath rest by Galilee,
O calm of hills above,
Where Jesus knelt to share with thee
The silence of eternity,
Interpreted by love!
Interpreted by love!

4.
Drop thy still dews of quietness,
Till all our strivings cease;
Take from our souls the strain and stress,
And let our ordered lives confess
The beauty of thy peace.
The beauty of thy peace.

5.
Breathe through the heats of our desire
Thy coolness and thy balm;
Let sense be dumb, let flesh retire;
Speak through the earthquake, wind, and fire,
O still, small voice of calm.
O still, small voice of calm.

And after the earthquake a fire; but the Lord was not in the fire: and after the fire a still small voice.
1 Kings 19:12 King James Version (KJV)

9
Down By The Riverside

Traditional

Nation shall not lift up sword against nation, neither shall they learn war any more.

Isaiah 2:4

10
From Heaven You Came
The Servant King

Graham Kendrick

There in the garden of tears,
My heavy load he chose to bear;
His heart with sorrow was torn,
'Yet not my will but yours,' he said.
This is our God, the Servant King,
He calls us now to follow him,
To bring our lives as a daily offering
Of worship to the Servant King.

Come, see his hands and his feet,
The scars that speak of sacrifice,
Hands that flung stars into space
To cruel nails surrendered.
This is our God, the Servant King,
He calls us now to follow him,
To bring our lives as a daily offering
Of worship to the Servant King.

So let us learn how to serve,
And in our lives enthrone him;
Each other's needs to prefer,
For it is Christ we're serving.
This is our God, the Servant King,
He calls us now to follow him,
To bring our lives as a daily offering
Of worship to the Servant King.

Copyright © 1983 Thankyou Music
(Adm. by Capitol CMG Publishing excl. UK & Europe, adm. by Integrity Music, part of the David C Cook family, songs@integritymusic.com)

ARTHUR'S THOUGHT FOR THE DAY
BIRTHDAYS

We all know and celebrate our birthdays but the Bible says "You must be born again" (John 3 vs 3). My second birthday was in 1935 before my confirmation and my decision to devote my life to God. It was not a sudden experience like St Paul on the road to Damascus or Newton, the slave trader during a storm.

When I celebrated my 95th birthday it was put in the weekly information sheet (at Abbots Leigh Manor Nursing Home). At a party, given by Paul and Lois, I had many visitors including some relatives that I had not seen for years. Some of their journeys were long and tiring and many brought presents.

When Christ was born wise men travelled from the East bearing gifts and shepherds, dazzled by the angels, left their sheep and travelled to Bethlehem to worship Jesus. (See also hymns 4, 5, 20 and 22).

12
How Great Thou Art

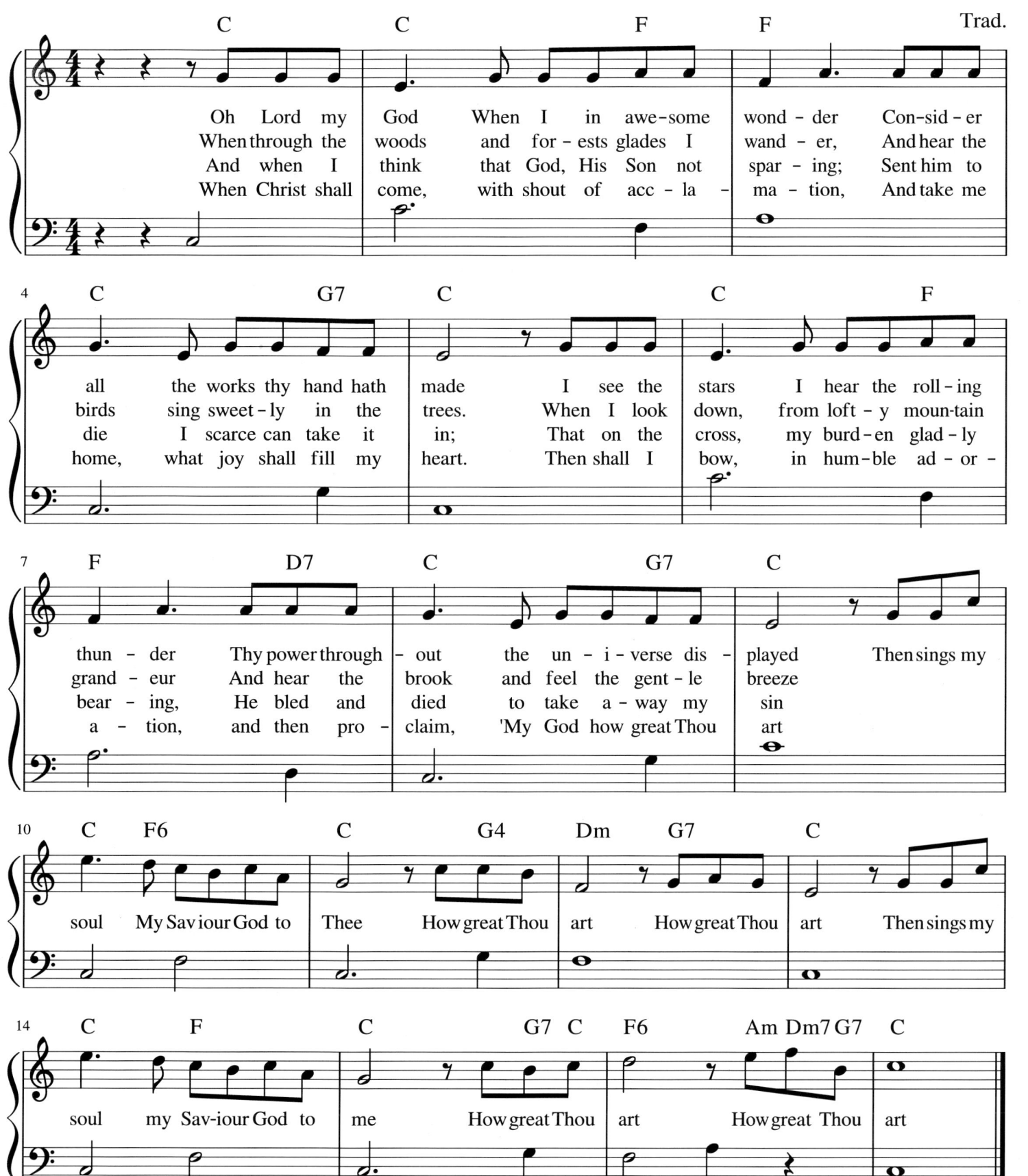

ARTHUR'S THOUGHT FOR THE DAY
GOD'S GREATNESS

One time on tour with the Male Voice Praise Choir we were in the Rockies in Canada with woods all round. Quite spontaneously a group started singing *How Great Thou Art* and we all joined in. It was a wonderful inspiring experience and that hymn now always reminds me of the occasion. (See the Frontispiece, page iv)

"Are not five sparrows sold for two cents? Yet not one of them is forgotten before God."
Luke 12:6

14
How Sweet the Name of Jesus Sounds

J. Newton 1779 A Reinagle 1836

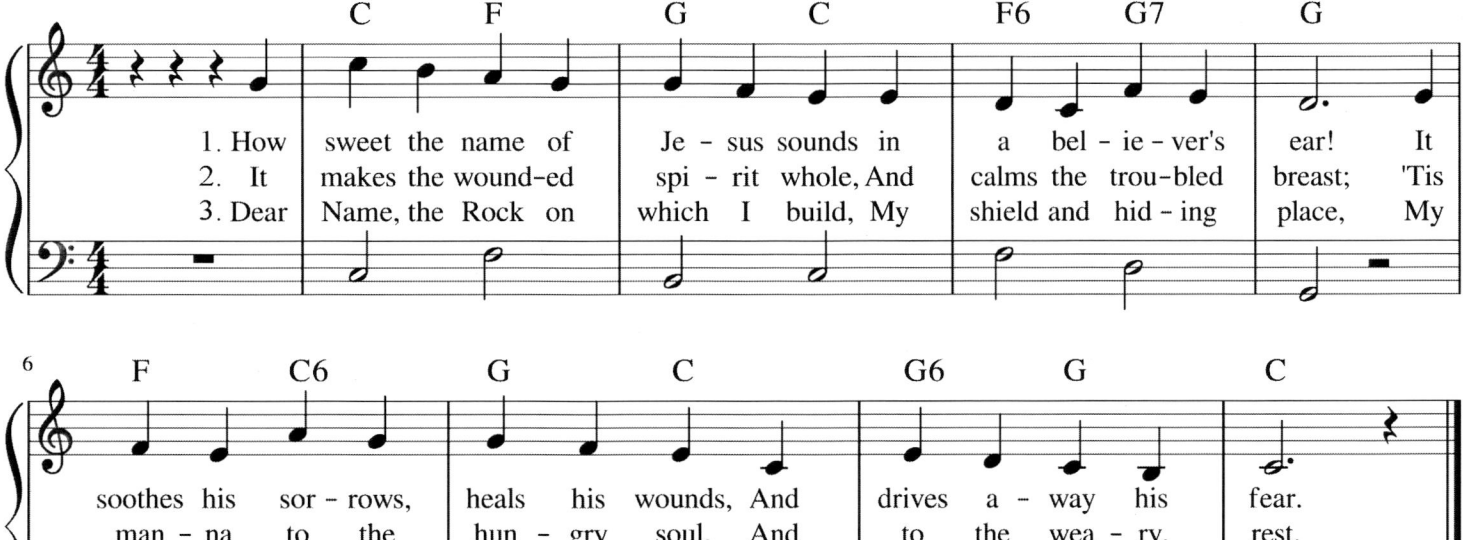

1. How sweet the name of Jesus sounds in a believer's ear! It soothes his sorrows, heals his wounds, And drives away his fear.

2. It makes the wounded spirit whole, And calms the troubled breast; 'Tis manna to the hungry soul, And to the weary, rest.

3. Dear Name, the Rock on which I build, My shield and hiding place, My never failing treasury, filled With boundless stores of grace!

4. By you my prayers acceptance gain
Although with sin defiled.
The devil charges me in vain,
And God calls me his child.

5. O Jesus, shepherd, guardian, friend,
My Prophet, Priest, and King,
My Lord, my life, my way, my end,
Accept the praise I bring.

6. Weak is the effort of my heart
How cold my warmest thought!
But when I see Thee as Thou art,
I'll praise Thee as I ought.

7. Till then I would your love proclaim
With every fleeting breath;
And may the music of your name
Refresh my soul in death!

ARTHUR'S THOUGHT FOR THE DAY:
TEN TITLES FOR JESUS

For spiritual growth we need to spend time daily in quiet meditation and communion with our Lord. John Newton, the ex-slave trader (see Amazing Grace, hymn number 1), has given us an excellent example for this reaching a crescendo in the fifth verse listing ten titles for Jesus:
Shepherd, Guardian, Friend, my Prophet, Priest, and King, my Lord, my Life, my Way, my End.
In verses six and seven Newton realises that Christian Praise will always be inadequate but we must never cease trying.

Newton was preaching one of his final sermons and, because of poor eyesight, had to be helped in the pulpit. He twice read *"Jesus Christ is precious"* and the helper said *"Go on, you have said that twice."* Newton replied "I have said it twice and I'll say it again."
The rafters rang as he shouted; *"Jesus Christ is precious".*

(Story from Amazing Grace, 366 Inspiring Hymns Stories for Daily Devotions by Kenneth W. Osbeck, Second Edition, Kregel Publications)

15
Just A Closer Walk With Thee

Traditional

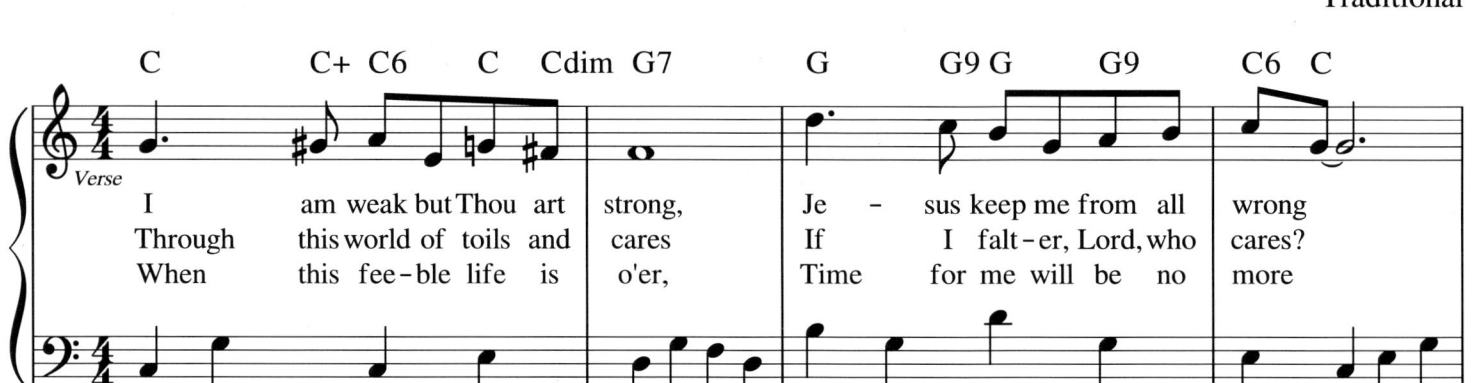

I am weak but Thou art strong, Jesus keep me from all wrong
Through this world of toils and cares, If I falter, Lord, who cares?
When this feeble life is o'er, Time for me will be no more

I'll be satisfied as long as I walk, let me walk, close to Thee.
Who with me my burden shares? None but Thee, Dear Lord, none but Thee
Guide me gently, safely home To thy Kingdom's shore to Thy shore

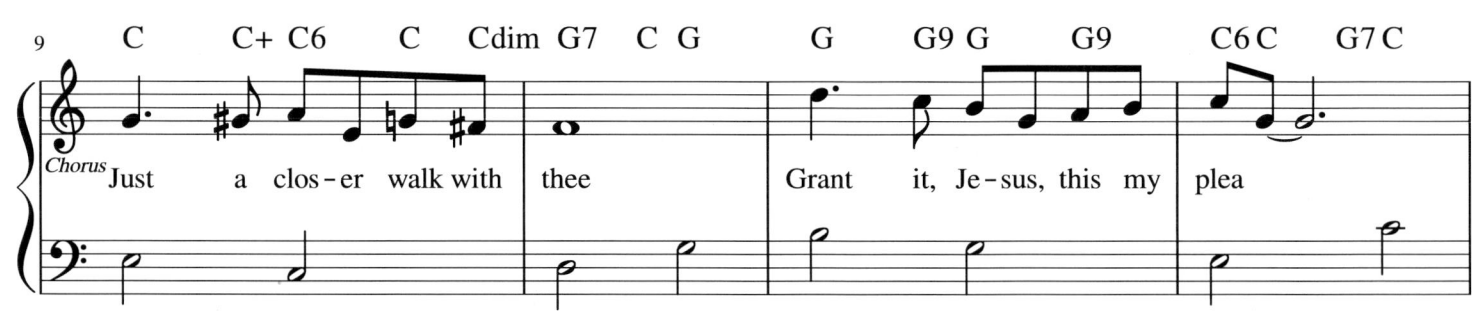

Chorus Just a closer walk with thee Grant it, Jesus, this my plea

Daily walking close to thee, Let it be, dear Lord, let it be.

Come near to God and he will come near to you. James 4:8 New International Version (NIV)

For we walk by faith, not by sight. 2 Corinthians 5:7 King James Version (KJV)

16
Love Makes It Easy

P Goddard

Paul Goddard

I was sailing in-to the dol-drums Diving so deep in des-pair Love came and saved me
Love is never as good as this, in any of the books that I read. You are all that I want-ed

Showed me that you were there. (All to geth er) Love makes it eas - y loving you the way that I do
You are all that I need

Love makes it eas - y Love has made my dreams come true. My life was in tor-ment un-

til the day I met you. love came and en - slaved me Can't stop loving you. (All to gether) Love makes it

eas - y loving you the way that I do Love makes it eas - y Love has made my dreams come true.

Make your face shine on your servant; save me in your steadfast love! Psalm 31:16
(See also Hymn 17)

17
Love Comes Shining Through

P Goddard

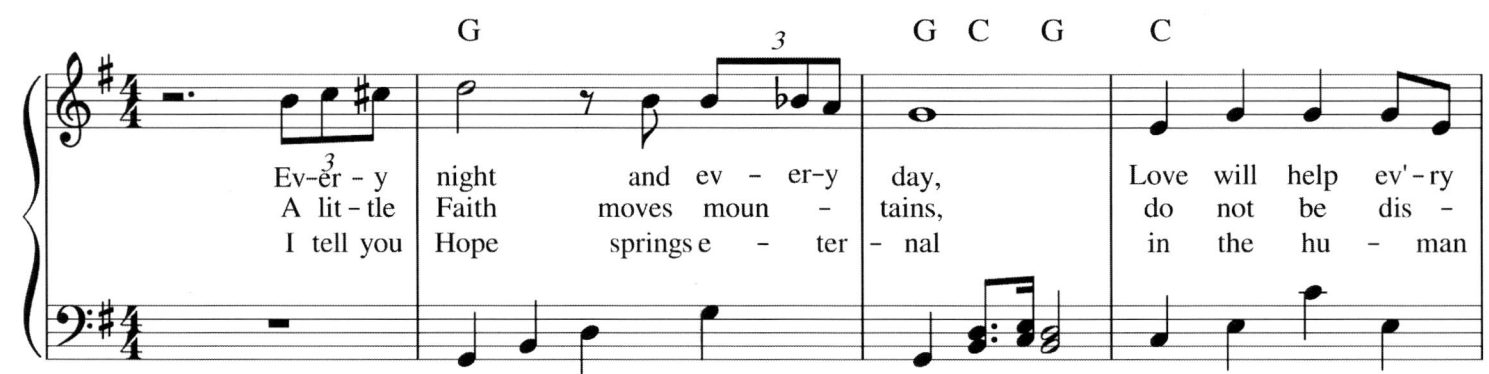
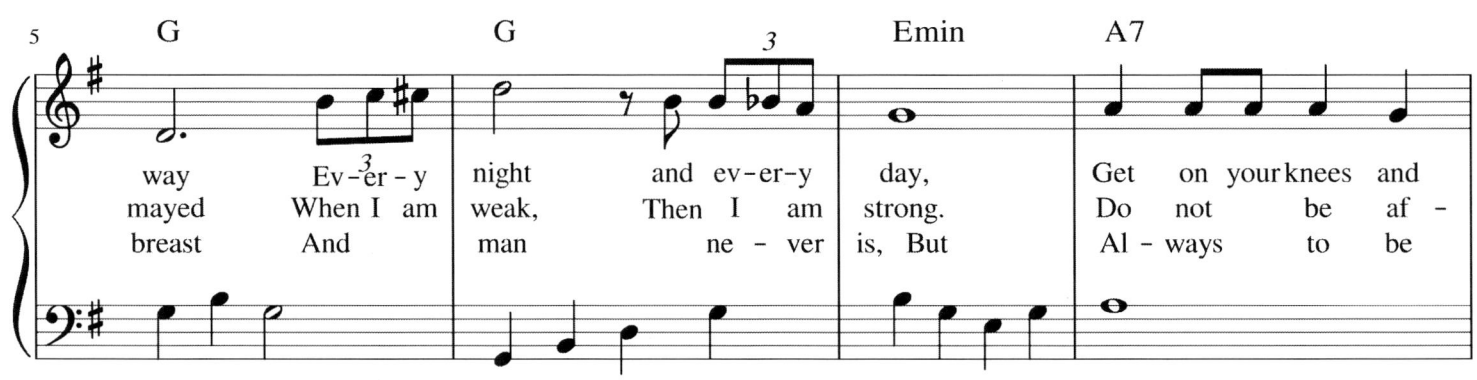

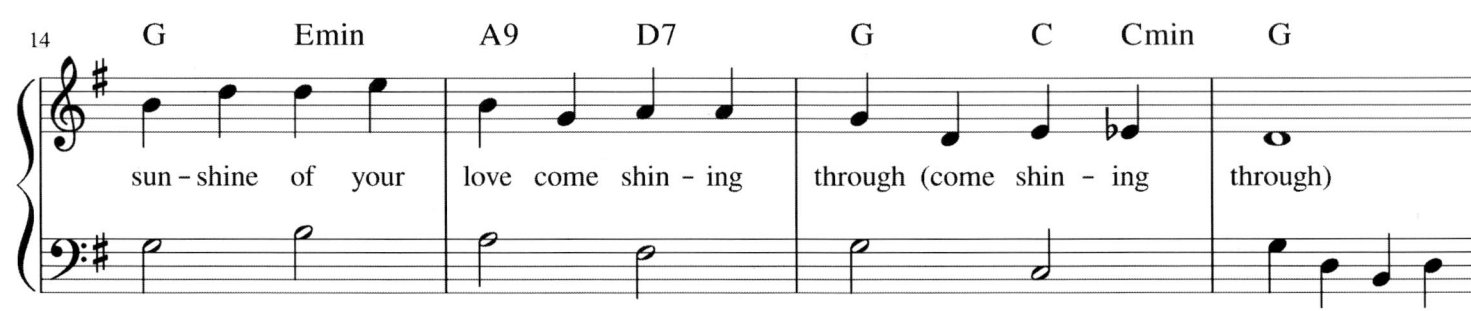

EDITOR'S NOTE

Arthur enjoyed hearing our band, Dr Jazz, play and they have played in Abbots Leigh on many occasions. This spiritual hymn was composed by the editor (Paul Goddard) for a concert by Dr. Jazz, the fund-raising band, at St Andrew's Church, Chew Stoke, in June 2017. The concert was a charity event sponsored by the Reverend Dr. Victor Barley and the funds went towards the restoration of the organ.

The original inspiration of this Hymn comes from 1 Corinthians chapter 13 verse 13:
"Three things will last forever--faith, hope, and love--and the greatest of these is love."
(New Living Translation).
Verse 3 of the hymn is from Alexander Pope, *An Essay on Man*

18
Michael Row The Boat Ashore

Traditional

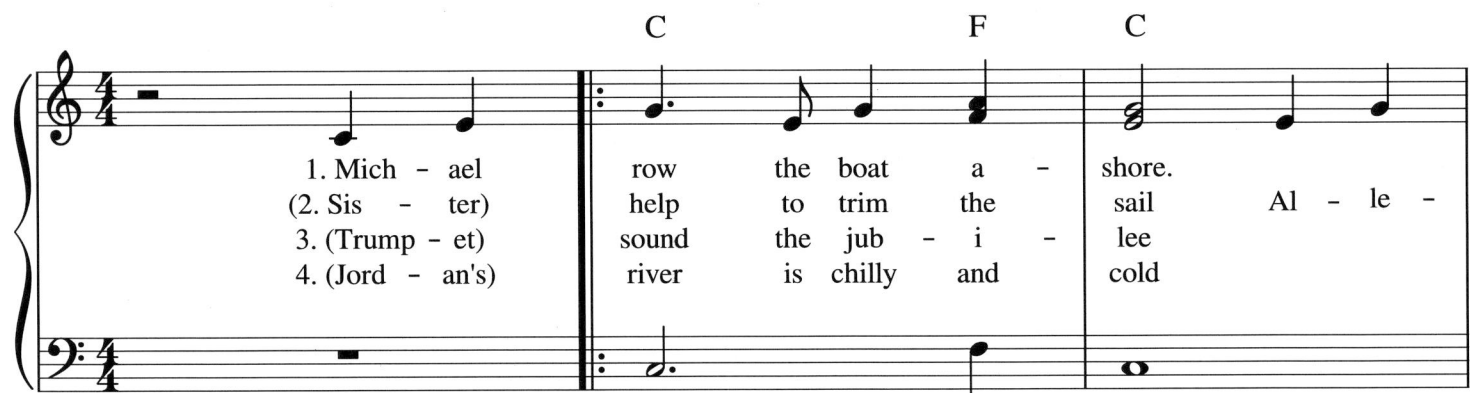
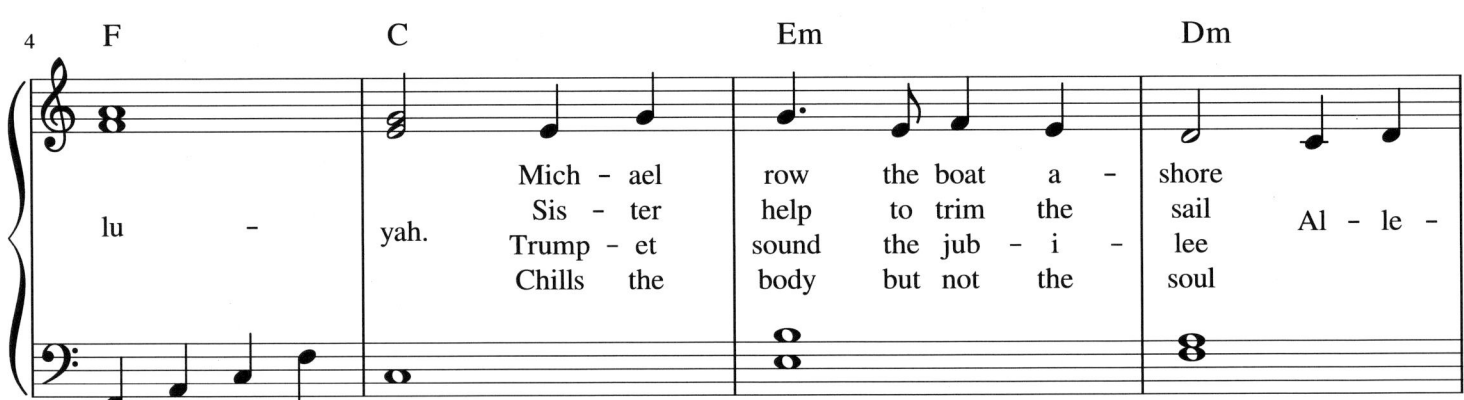
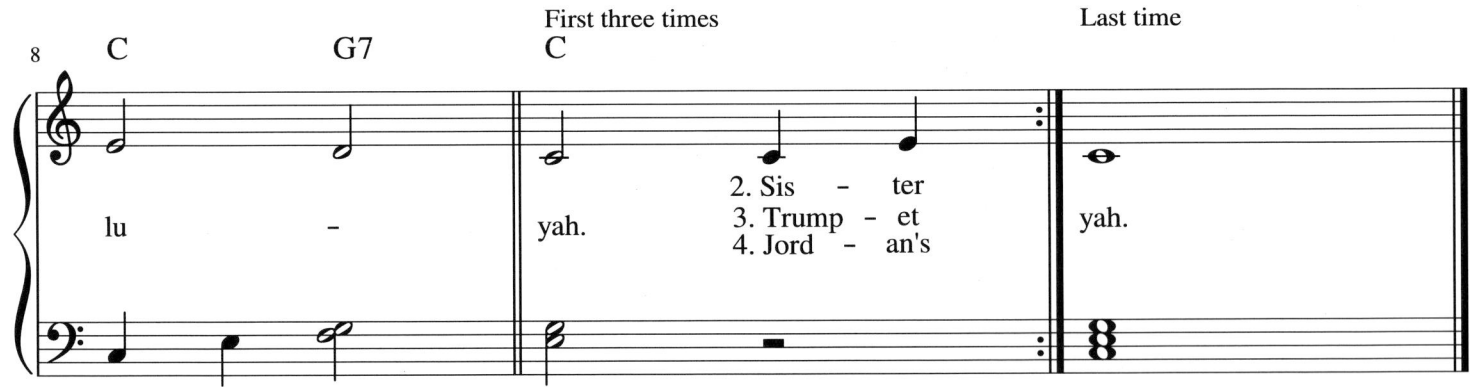

In a moment, in the twinkling of an eye, at the last trump: for the trumpet shall sound,
and the dead shall be raised incorruptible, and we shall be changed.
1 Corinthians 15:52 (KJV)

19
Nobody Know The Trouble I've Seen

Traditional

20
Oh Little Town of Bethlehem

Phillips Brooks 1835-93 Traditional

2. For Christ is born of Mary
   And gathered all above
   While mortals sleep, the angels keep
   Their watch of wondering love
   O morning stars together
   Proclaim the holy birth
   And praises sing to God the King
   And Peace to men on earth

3. How silently, how silently
   The wondrous gift is given!
   So God imparts to human hearts
   The blessings of His heaven.
   No ear may hear His coming,
   But in this world of sin,
   Where meek souls will receive him still,
   The dear Christ enters in

4. O holy Child of Bethlehem
   Descend to us, we pray
   Cast out our sin and enter in
   Be born to us today
   We hear the Christmas angels
   The great glad tidings tell
   O come to us, abide with us
   Our Lord Emmanuel

So Joseph also went up from the town of Nazareth in Galilee to Judea, to Bethlehem the town of David, because he belonged to the house and line of David.
Luke 2:4 New International Version (NIV)

21
Oh When The Saints
Go Marching In

Traditional

ARTHUR'S THOUGHT FOR THE DAY:
WHO IS A SAINT?

A saint has been described by someone as a Christian who makes it easier for others to believe in God: every believer whom God has sanctified by his Spirit and who has been called to sainthood.

We should thankfully remember in Christian fellowship those who have already been called to their heavenly home. We should also thank God for any particular person or group who have specially influenced our lives directing us to God.

But how do we best honour the memory of others who have contributed to our lives? By rededicating our life to God, obeying Him implictly and reaching out to help others.

23
Swing Low, Sweet Chariot

*"Jordan's river is chilly and wide
But there is milk and honey on the other side."*
THE MILK OF THE WORD
(excerpt from one of Arthur's <u>short</u> talks)

A clergyman was invited to give a sermon at a neighbouring church. As the parson and the verger were leaving the vestry to start the service the verger looked flustered.

'You've forgotten your notes,' he remarked to the parson.

'Goodness me,' replied the vicar. 'I don't use notes. I use inspiration.'

The sermon went on for a very long time, the clergyman preaching in a rambling way on the text from 1 Peter Chapter 2, verses 1 and 2. *"Wherefore laying aside all malice, and all guile, and hypocrisies, and envies, and all evil speakings, as newborn babes, desire the sincere milk of the word, that ye may grow thereby."*

After the service and back in the vestry the parson turned to the verger.

'How did I do?' he enquired.

'Well,' replied the verger. 'We do like the milk of the word but we like it condensed.'

25
The Lord's My Shepherd

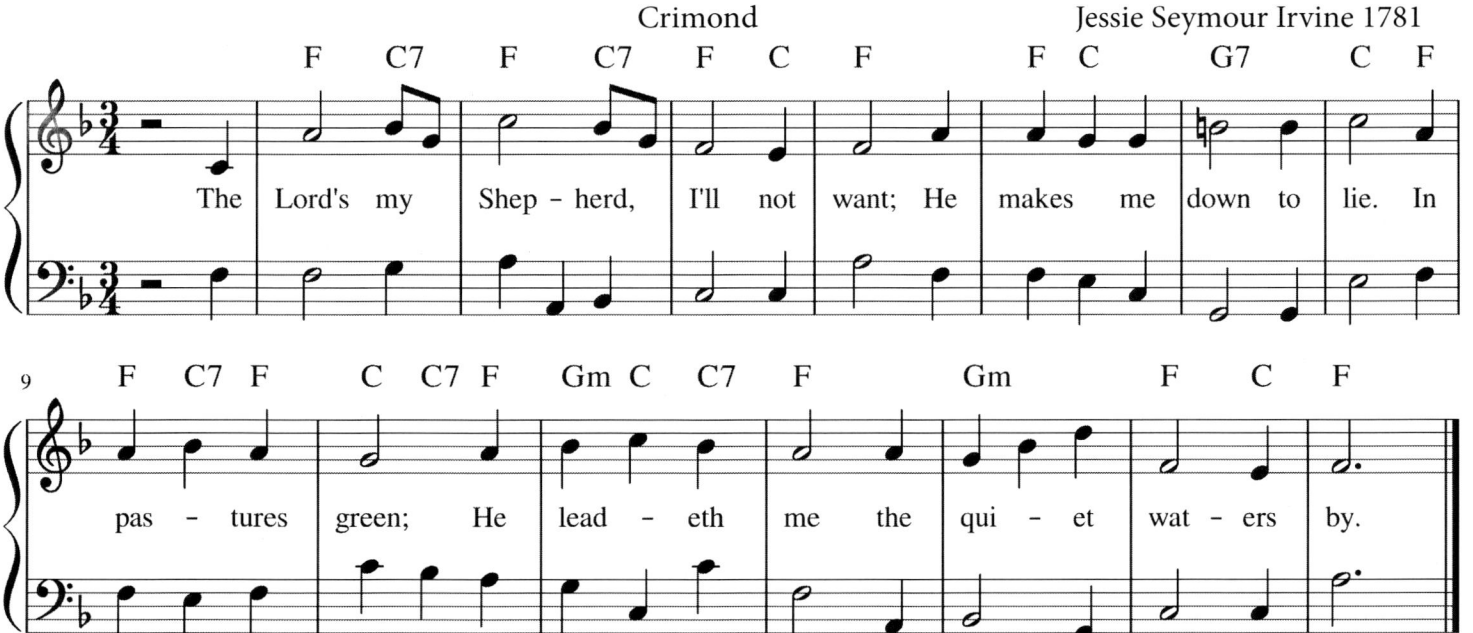

Crimond
Jessie Seymour Irvine 1781

The Lord's my Shep-herd, I'll not want; He makes me down to lie. In pas-tures green; He lead-eth me the qui-et wat-ers by.

2. My soul he doth restore again,
And me to walk doth make
Within the paths of righteousness,
E'en for his own name's sake.

3. Yea, though I walk in death's dark vale,
Yet will I fear no ill:
For thou art with me, and thy rod
And staff me comfort still.

4. My table thou hast furnished
In presence of my foes;
My head thou dost with oil anoint
And my cup overflows.

5. Goodness and mercy all my life
Shall surely follow me;
And in God's house for evermore
My dwelling-place shall be.

ARTHUR'S THOUGHT FOR THE DAY:
SHEPHERDS AND THEIR SHEEP

Hymns 25 and 26 are very faithful to Psalm 23
The Lord is my shepherd; I shall not want. He maketh me to lie down in green pastures: he leadeth me beside the still waters. He restoreth my soul: he leadeth me in the paths of righteousness for his name's sake. Yea, though I walk through the valley of the shadow of death, I will fear no evil: for thou art with me; thy rod and thy staff they comfort me. Thou preparest a table before me in the presence of mine enemies: thou anointest my head with oil; my cup runneth over. Surely goodness and mercy shall follow me all the days of my life: and I will dwell in the house of the Lord for ever

At the rear of the house, here at Abbotts Leigh Manor, we can usually see some sheep peacefully grazing in the large field. In our Lord's day the sheep were kept in a shelter at night, safe from the wolves and from any robbers. But there was no door. The shepherd slept in the doorway....Jesus said *"I am the door; if anyone enters through Me, he shall be saved, and shall go in and out, and find pasture."* (John 10:9)." and then in verse 11 *"I am the good shepherd. The good shepherd lays down his life for the sheep."*

(See also hymns 2 and 30)

26
The King of Love

Henry William Baker (1821-77)   John Bacchus Dykes (1823-76)

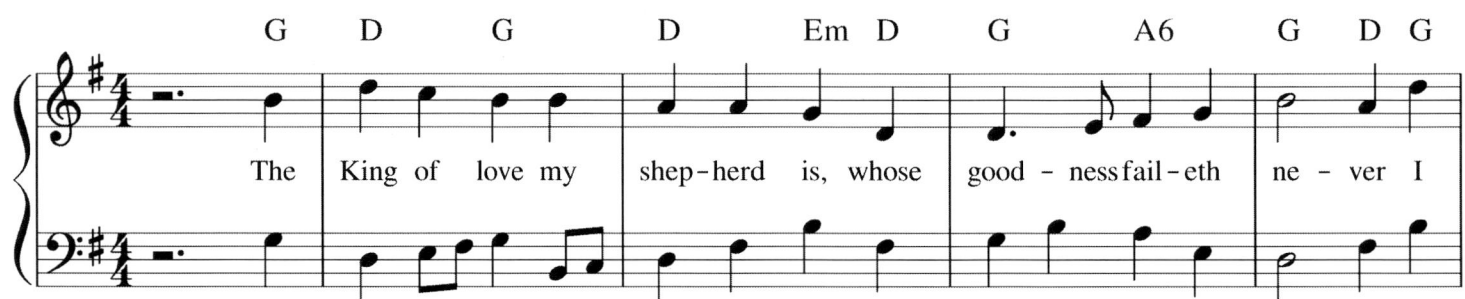

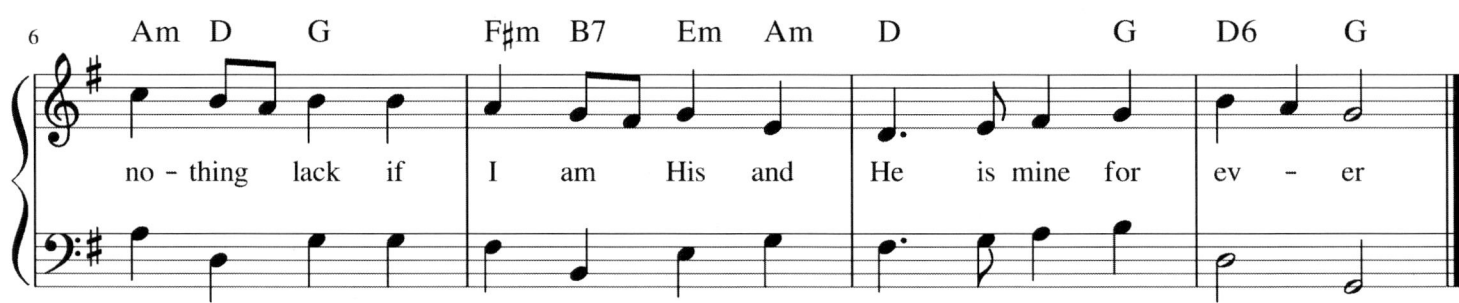

2. Where streams of living water flow,
My ransomed soul he leadeth
And, where the verdant pastures grow,
With food celestial feedeth.

3. Perverse and foolish oft I strayed,
But yet in love he sought me
And on his shoulder gently laid
And home rejoicing brought me.

4. In death's dark vale I fear no ill
With thee, dear Lord, beside me,
Thy rod and staff my comfort still,
Thy cross before to guide me.

5. Thou spredst a table in my sight;
Thine unction grace bestoweth;
And, oh, what transport of delight
From thy pure chalice floweth!

6. And so through all the length of days
Thy goodness faileth never.
Good Shepherd, may I sing thy praise
Within thy house forever.

27
The Old Rugged Cross

George Bennard 1873-1958

Arr. P. Goddard 2015

28
There Is A Green Hill

Text: Cecil Frances Alexander, 1818-1895 Music: John H. Gower, 1855-1922

2. We may not know, we cannot tell,
What pains he had to bear,
But we believe it was for us
He hung and suffered there.

3. There was no other good enough
To pay the price of sin.
He only could unlock the gate
Of heav'n and let us in.

4. Oh, dearly, dearly has he loved!
And we must love him too,
And trust in his redeeming blood,
And try his works to do.

ARTHUR'S THOUGHT FOR THE DAY: GREEN HILLS

When my son Paul visited me recently we sat in the first floor lounge and discussed what would be the subject of my 'Thought for the Day' for the next Sunday. The weather was good and the visibility excellent. Beyond the Bristol Channel the green hills of Wales were very clear.

'Why not talk about some of our experiences in Wales,' Paul suggested.

My first visit to Wales was in 1938. I was with nine of my friends in a chauffeur driven Buick. At the first sight of the mountains I was hooked. We joined a tented camp with about three hundred young people on a farm just south of Barmouth. We had a wonderful time climbing up Snowdon and also reaching the summit of Cader Idris where a violent thunderstorm broke and we were drenched in no time. I shall never forget the lightening and thunder and rain all round us! My second visit was in August 1939. We had a small car and my brother and I drove... a much quieter journey!

Years passed. I spent six years in the army and returned to my job as an estate agent, now married to Grace. Sydney, my brother, went to a theological college and was ordained. He was a vicar and then a canon in the Liverpool area and visited Wales often. He bought a derelict farmhouse called Gwynfynydd near Trawsfynydd in the Snowdonia National Park. After much work on the property he arranged for groups of young people from Liverpool slums to have holidays in the farmhouse. Most of them had never seen a live sheep or cow and they were awestruck by the mountains!

During the 1960s Grace and I organised groups of twenty (or more) young people from South Croydon to holiday at Gwynfynydd. We had a suitable person as a chaplain and enjoyed wonderful fellowship every evening and by day saw the wonder of God's creation all round us.

Eventually we bought a cottage in Trawsfynydd village and Sydney and Cicely retired to a nearby hamlet. We visited Trawsfynydd as often as we could until Grace was ill and we sold the cottage.

How I miss our visits to the Welsh mountains! But I was privileged on four occasions to join a gospel male voice choir tour of Canada and the United States of America....including tours through the Rockies and Niagara Falls ... wonders of creation indeed!

Psalm 121 King James Version (KJV)
1. I will lift up mine eyes unto the hills, from whence cometh my help.
2 My help cometh from the Lord, which made heaven and earth

Please see also Hymn 12, (How Great Thou Art) and the Frontispiece on page iv.

29
There Will Be Peace In The Valley

Thomas A Dorsey

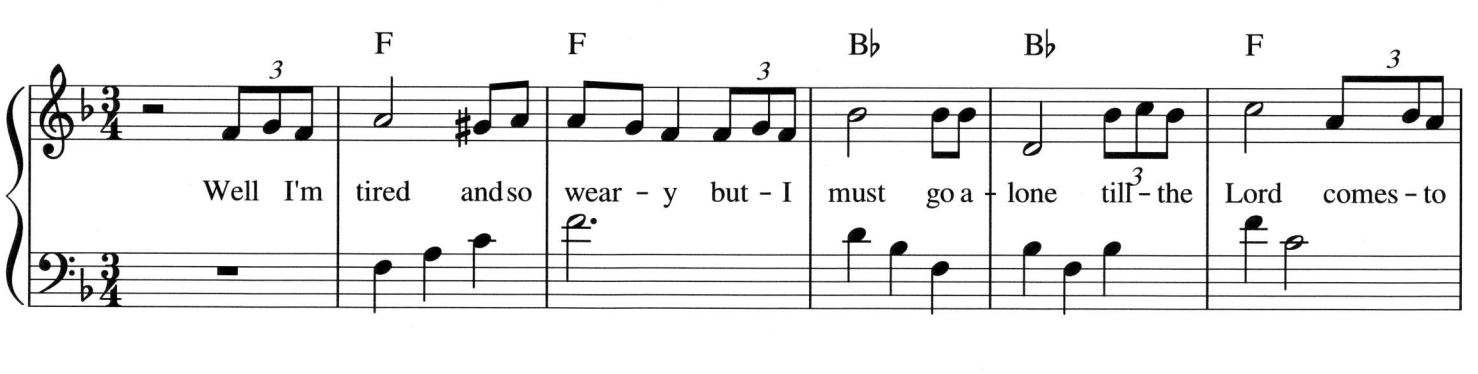

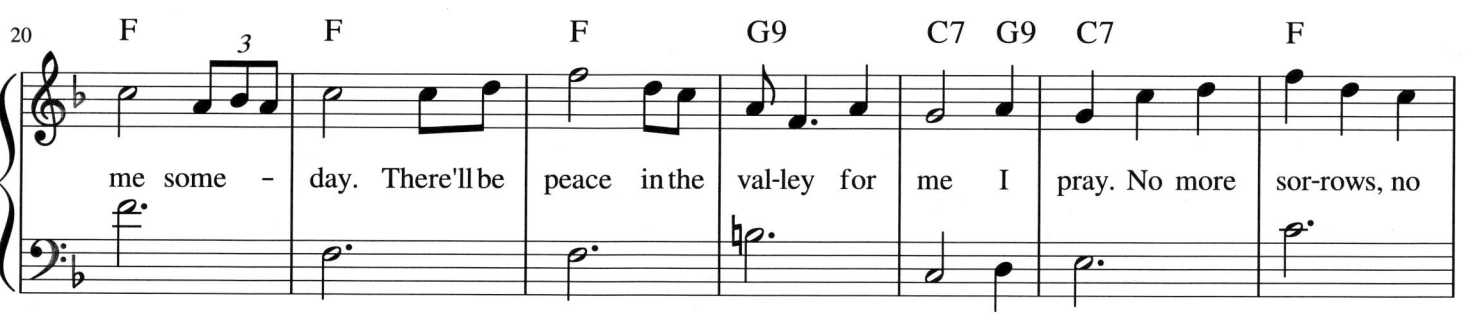

EDITOR'S NOTE: *Peace in the Valley* was included because of its association with Elvis Presley after he sang it on the Ed Sullivan show. Elvis received three Grammy Awards for his gospel recordings. Arthur particularly enjoyed visiting Elvis's home Graceland with the Male Voice Praise choir on tour.

30
There Were Ninety and Nine

2. Lord, Thou hast here Thy ninety and nine;
   Are they not enough for Thee?"
   But the Shepherd made answer: "This of Mine
   Has wandered away from Me;
   And although the road be rough and steep,
   I go to the desert to find My sheep,
   I go to the desert to find My sheep."

3. But none of the ransomed ever knew
   How deep were the waters crossed;
   Nor how dark was the night the Lord passed through
   Ere He found His sheep that was lost.
   Out in the desert He heard its cry,
   Sick and helpless and ready to die;
   Sick and helpless and ready to die.

4. "Lord, whence are those blood drops all the way
   That mark out the mountain's track?"
   "They were shed for one who had gone astray
   Ere the Shepherd could bring him back."
   "Lord, whence are Thy hands so rent and torn?"
   "They are pierced tonight by many a thorn;
   They are pierced tonight by many a thorn."

5. And all through the mountains, thunder riven
   And up from the rocky steep,
   There arose a glad cry to the gate of Heaven,
   "Rejoice! I have found My sheep!"
   And the angels echoed around the throne,
   "Rejoice, for the Lord brings back His own!

31
Thou Didst Leave Thy Throne
(O come to my heart, Lord Jesus)

Emily Elliot 1864   T R Matthews

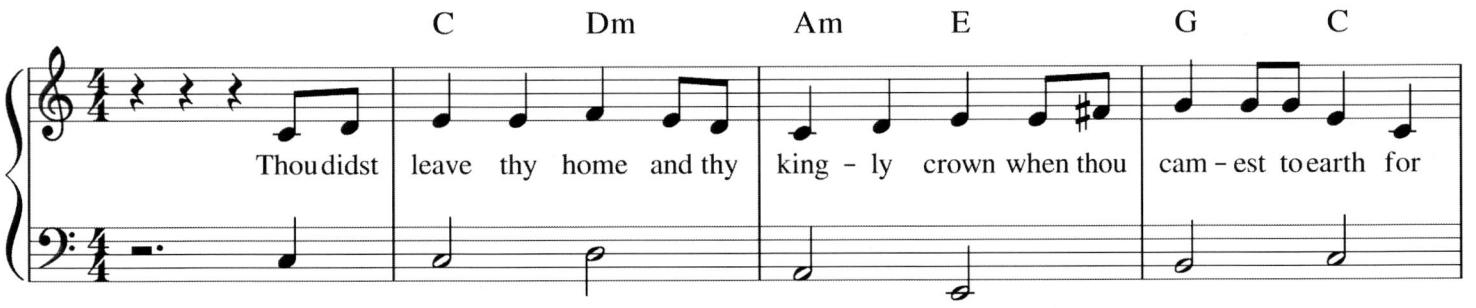

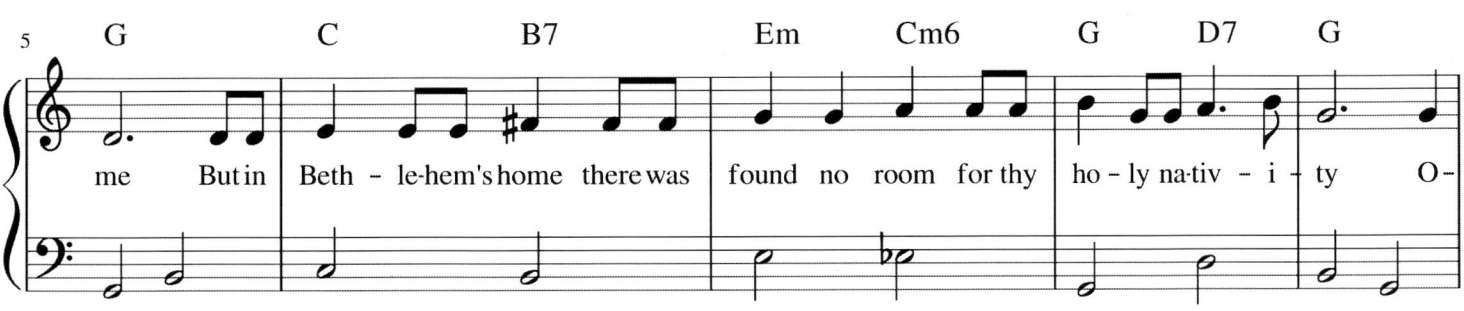

2. Heaven's arches rang when the angels sang,
Proclaiming Thy royal degree;
But of lowly birth didst Thou come to earth,
And in great humility.
O come to my heart, Lord Jesus,
There is room in my heart for Thee.

3. The foxes found rest, and the birds their nest
In the shade of the forest tree;
But Thy couch was the sod, O Thou Son of God,
In the deserts of Galilee.
O come to my heart, Lord Jesus,
There is room in my heart for Thee.

4. Thou camest, O Lord, with the living Word,
That should set Thy people free;
But with mocking scorn and with crown of thorn,
They bore Thee to Calvary.
O come to my heart, Lord Jesus,
There is room in my heart for Thee.

5. When the heav'ns shall ring, and her choirs shall sing,
At Thy coming to victory,
Let Thy voice call me home, saying "Yet there is room,
There is room at My side for thee."
My heart shall rejoice, Lord Jesus,
When Thou comest and callest for me.

32
Wade In The Water

Traditional

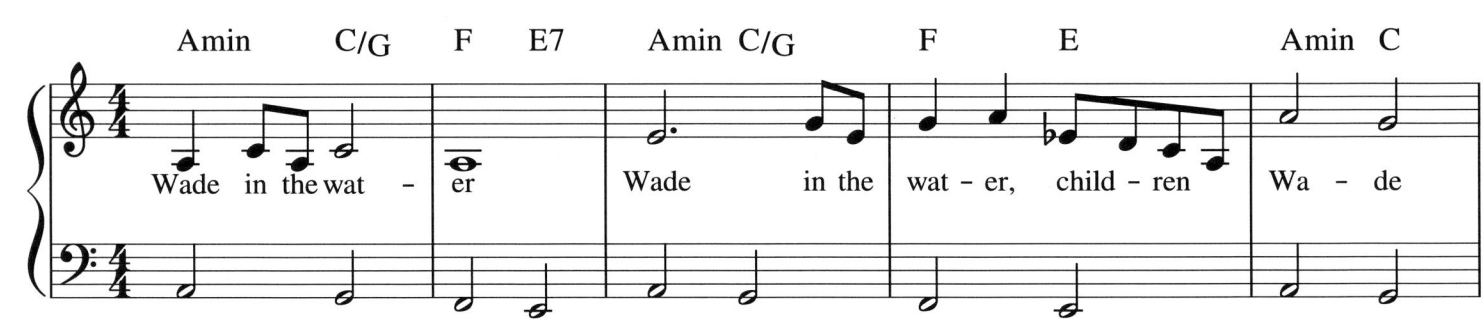
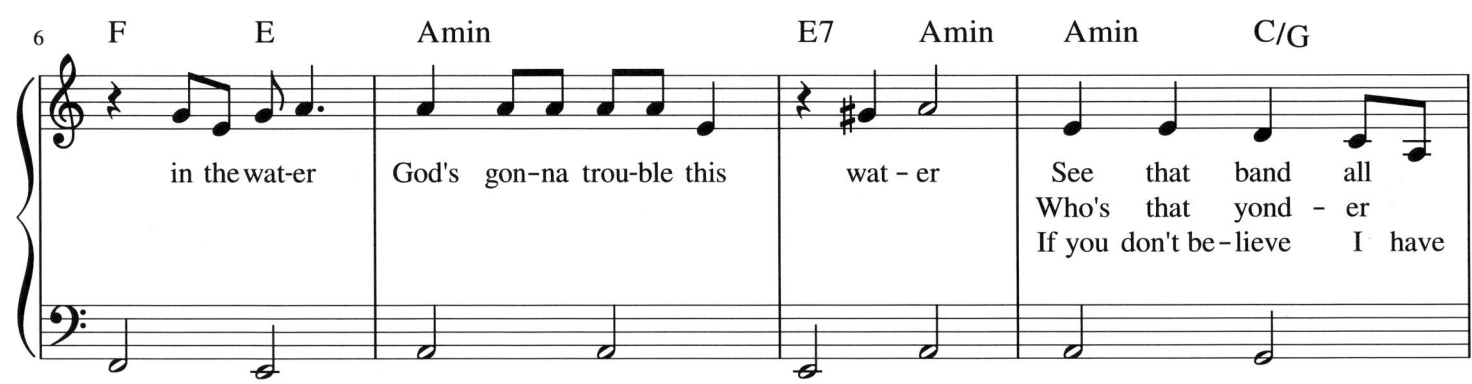
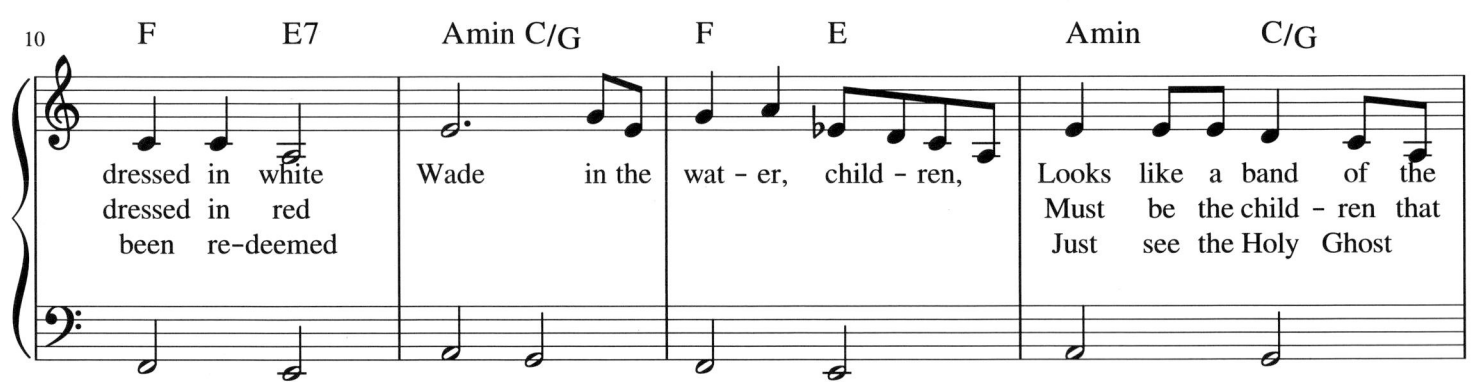
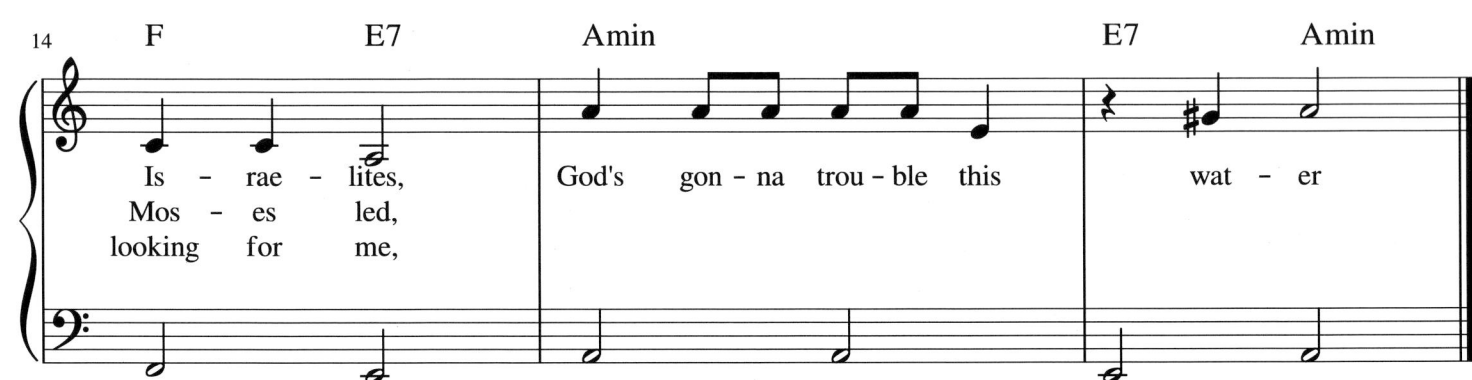

33
We Have An Anchor

EDITOR'S NOTE: *THE BOY'S BRIGADE HYMN*
This hymn, written by Priscilla Owens (1829–1907) of Maryland US, has always been associated with the Boy's Brigade. Arthur was, for many years, a leader of the Boy's Brigade at Christ Church, Broadmead, West Croydon and this was one of his firm favourites.

34
What A Friend We Have In Jesus

Joseph M Scriven 1855 Charles C Converse 1868

ARTHUR'S THOUGHT FOR THE DAY:
FRIENDS

True friends love us as we are, stay close when times are good or bad and are always ready in time of need. Joseph Scriven lived in Ireland leading a very pleasant life of good health, wealth and education. He was a member of a devoted family then tragedy struck. The night before they were to be wed Joseph's fiancée accidentally drowned. Scriven found solace in Jesus, he dramatically changed his life style and left Ireland for Canada to devote his life to helping others. In Ontario he became known as the Good Samaritan of Port Hope.

Scriven's mother became ill in Ireland and he wrote a comforting letter enclosing "a new poem" to remind her of a never failing heavenly friend. Later Scriven himself was ill and a neighbour, sitting up with him, noticed a copy of it on a scrap of paper. The neighbour asked who had written the beautiful words and Scriven replied "The Lord and I together wrote the poem."

A copy was taken to a music publisher and a tune was written by an American lawyer, Charles Converse. The great American evangelist Dwight L. Moody thought it was the most touching modern hymn he had ever heard. It has constantly been in the list of top ten favourite hymns.

35
When I Survey The Wondrous Cross

Isaac Watts(1674-1748) E. Miller (1731-1807)

37

ARTHUR'S THOUGHT FOR THE DAY:
SURVEYING

I spent my working life as a chartered surveyor and perhaps you would be interested in a few words about surveying.

What is the definition of a survey? The dictionary says: *"To view comprehensively and extensively. To examine in detail."*

There are several purposes of a survey: Prior to constructing a building it enables the preparation of plans and supervision of construction. Surveying of existing buildings for building societies, banks, local authorities and insurance companies is carried out for the purpose of a mortgage.

Private surveys are carried out for a purchaser's benefit so that they may be aware of the conditions of the property before purchase.

The purpose of the survey determines the scope. The survey for a building society is to safeguard the body lending the money and its main purpose is valuation. A survey for a purchaser is more detailed and the report is submitted to him or her. A private survey should look at the general structural condition and examine parts of the building not usually accessible to a purchaser.

Method of procedure:

- General impression of the house externally and internally and note of accommodation
- Inspect the roof void, the timbers, tanks and insulation.
- Proceed room by room measuring and taking notes.
- Examine the cellar, if there is one.
- Check for rising damp.
- Look at outbuildings, garage etc.
- Check all main walls, paintwork and fences.
- Test the drainage.
- Test the electrical installation

Timber

Inspecting the timber of a property is an important part of a surveyor's work.

With regard to timber the surveyor must particularly look for woodworm, wet rot, weevil and dry rot.

Dry rot is particularly nasty. Nearly invisible mycelia strands stretch out to feed on timber and eventually a fruiting body will be produced and rupture, spreading millions of tiny spores into the atmosphere every hour!

There is much more that can be said but that's just a taster on surveying.

Covenant

There is, however, one defect that most houses have and the surveyor cannot see by surveying the house. That is a mortgage! This is a covenant. The debt is stated and terms of repayment detailed. The repayment is the Redemption. There are, of course, penalties for not complying.

In a similar way God has made a covenant or promise to each of us individually. But each one of us has failed to comply. *"For all have sinned, and come short of the glory of God"* Romans 3:23 King James Version (KJV).

Once the debt to the building society has been paid the society has to acknowledge that they have all the money due and the debt has been redeemed.

Christ has paid our debt to God in full *"For the wages of sin is death; but the gift of God is eternal life through Jesus Christ our Lord."* Roman 6. 23 (KJV).

> *When I survey the wondrous Cross*
> *On which the Prince of Glory died*
> *My richest gain, I count but loss*
> *And pour contempt on all my pride*

Often the houses that I surveyed were occupied but sometimes they were empty. On one occasion when the key opened the door of an empty house I did not dare step inside. The house was literally falling into a hole and was exceedingly dangerous. It put me in mind of Matthew 7. 27 :

"And the rain descended, and the floods came, and the winds blew, and beat upon that house; and it fell: and great was the fall of it."

In one empty house I checked the bathroom door. It closed perfectly but jammed and, despite my best efforts, would not open. I was trapped on the inside! Fortunately a builder was inspecting the house with me and heard me calling for assistance so I was let out.

An open door provides opportunities. In God's plan in our lives he encourages us to open the door. Revelation 3:20 King James Version (KJV):

"Behold, I stand at the door, and knock: if any man hear my voice, and open the door, I will come in to him, and will sup with him, and he with me."